SENSATIONAL STARTERS

Consultant Editor:
Valerie Ferguson

LORENZ BOOKS

Contents

Introduction

Starters should be regarded as the prelude to a meal. They are intended to tickle the palate and prepare it for the delights to come, to whet the appetite rather than to satisfy it.

For this reason, always choose a starter that complements or balances the main course in content, flavour and texture. One creamy dish followed by another is unlikely to prove a success. If your main dish is rich and substantial, opt for a light first course, and vice versa; and, obviously, avoid pairing starters and main courses based on the same ingredients.

Starters should also be visually as well as gastronomically appealing, and attractively served in small portions.

This book shows you how to prepare a variety of starters, both for everyday eating and for entertaining. There is something for each season of the year, from the stunningly colourful Papaya & Avocado Salad for hot summer days to Brandied Roquefort Tarts, perfect for chilly winter nights. Choose from simply made soups and refreshing salads, vegetarian options such as Sweetcorn Blinis with Dill Cream, or enjoy a touch of luxury with Oysters Rockefeller. Many of the recipes can be prepared in advance and are therefore excellent for entertaining.

Techniques

Preparing Chillies

1 Always protect your hands as chillies can irritate the skin; wear rubber gloves if possible, and never rub your eyes after handling chillies. Halve each chilli lengthways and remove and discard the fiery-hot seeds.

2 Slice and finely chop the chillies and use as required. Wash the knife and chopping board thoroughly in hot, soapy water. Always wash your hands carefully after you have been preparing chillies.

Peeling Sweet Peppers

As peppers have awkward curves, alternative methods of peeling, such as grilling, are best. This also intensifies the sweetness of the flesh.

1 Set the peppers on a rack in a grill pan and grill close to the heat. Turn the peppers to char and blister the skin all over. Alternatively, spear each pepper on a long-handled fork and hold it over a flame, turning it slowly so that the skin is charred and blistered on all sides.

2 Put the peppers in a plastic bag and tie it. Leave to cool; the steam trapped inside the bag will help loosen the skin. When the peppers are cool enough to handle, peel with a small knife.

Chopping Herbs

1 Place the leaves on a clean, dry board. Use a large, sharp cook's knife (if you use a blunt knife you will bruise the herbs rather than slice them) and chop them until as coarse or as fine as needed.

2 Alternatively, use a herb chopper, also called a *mezzaluna*, which is a very useful tool for finely chopping herbs or vegetables and consists of a sharp, curved blade with 2 handles. Use the *mezzaluna* in a see-saw motion for best results.

Blanching & Refreshing

Vegetables are blanched for several reasons: to loosen skins before peeling, to set colour and flavour, and to reduce bitterness. They are often blanched as an initial cooking, when further cooking is to be done by stir-frying or a brief reheating in butter, or if they are to be used in a salad. After blanching, most foods are "refreshed" to stop them cooking any further.

1 To blanch: immerse the food in a large pan of boiling water. Bring the water back to the boil and boil for the time specified, usually 1–2 minutes. Immediately lift the food out of the water or strain.

2 To refresh: quickly immerse the food in iced water or hold under cold running water. If the recipe specifies, leave until it has cooled completely. Drain well.

Asparagus Soup

This delicately flavoured soup is best made with young asparagus which is more tender and therefore blends well.

Serves 4

INGREDIENTS
450 g/1 lb young asparagus
40 g/1½ oz/3 tbsp butter
6 shallots, sliced
15 g/½ oz/2 tbsp plain flour
600 ml/1 pint/2½ cups vegetable stock
    or water
15 ml/1 tbsp lemon juice
250 ml/8 fl oz/1 cup milk
120 ml/4 fl oz/½ cup single cream
10 ml/2 tsp chopped fresh chervil,
    to serve
salt and freshly ground
    black pepper

1 Trim the stalks of the asparagus if necessary. Cut 4 cm/1½ in off the tops of half the asparagus and set aside. Slice the remaining asparagus.

2 Melt 25 g/1 oz/2 tbsp of the butter and gently fry the shallots for 2–3 minutes until they are soft but not browned.

3 Add the sliced asparagus and fry over a gentle heat for about 1 minute. Stir in the flour and cook for 1 minute. Stir in the stock or water, lemon juice and seasoning. Bring to the boil and then simmer, partially covered, for 15–20 minutes until the asparagus is very tender.

4 Cool slightly and then process the soup in a food processor or blender until smooth. Press through a sieve placed over a clean saucepan. Add the milk by pouring and stirring it through the sieve with the asparagus so as to extract the maximum amount of asparagus purée.

5 Melt the remaining butter and fry the reserved asparagus tips gently for about 3–4 minutes to soften. Heat the soup gently for 3–4 minutes, adding the cream and asparagus tips. Serve sprinkled with chervil.

Prawn Bisque

The classic French recipe for bisque requires pushing the shellfish through
a *tamis*, or drum sieve, which produces a velvet-smooth result.

Serves 6–8

INGREDIENTS
675 g/1½ lb small or medium cooked
   prawns in the shell
25 ml/1½ tbsp vegetable oil
2 onions, halved and sliced
1 large carrot, sliced
2 celery sticks, sliced
2 litres/3½ pints/8
   cups water
few drops of lemon juice
30 ml/2 tbsp tomato purée
1 bouquet garni
50 g/2 oz/4 tbsp butter
50 g/2 oz/½ cup plain flour
45–60 ml/3–4 tbsp brandy
150 ml/¼ pint/⅔ cup
   whipping cream
salt and freshly ground
   white pepper
flat leaf parsley,
   to garnish

1 Peel the prawns and reserve the
heads and shells for the stock.
Chill the peeled prawns.

2 Heat the oil, add the heads and
shells and cook over high heat, stirring
frequently, until starting to brown.

3 Reduce the heat, add the vegetables
and fry gently for about 5 minutes
until the onions start to soften.

4 Add the water, lemon juice, tomato
purée and bouquet garni. Bring to the
boil, cover and simmer gently for 25
minutes. Strain through a sieve.

5 Melt the butter over a medium
heat. Stir in the flour and cook until
just golden, stirring. Add the brandy
and gradually pour in about half the
stock, whisking until smooth, then
whisk in the rest. Season to taste.
Reduce the heat, cover and simmer
for 5 minutes, stirring frequently.

6 Strain the soup into a clean pan. Add the cream and a little extra lemon juice to taste, then stir in most of the reserved prawns and heat through, stirring. Serve garnished with the remaining prawns and parsley.

Classic French Onion Soup

When French onion soup is made slowly and carefully, the onions almost caramelize to a deep mahogany colour. The soup has a superb flavour and is a perfect winter supper dish.

Serves 4

INGREDIENTS
4 large onions
30 ml/2 tbsp sunflower or olive oil,
    or 15 ml/1 tbsp of each
25 g/1 oz/2 tbsp butter
900 ml/1½ pints/3¾ cups
    beef stock
4 slices French bread
40–50 g/1½–2 oz Gruyère or Cheddar
    cheese, grated
salt and freshly ground
    black pepper

1 Peel and quarter the onions and slice or chop them into 5 mm/¼ in pieces. Heat the oil and butter together in a deep, heavy-based saucepan, preferably with a medium-size base so that the onions form a thick layer.

COOK'S TIP: At first the onions need to be stirred only occasionally, but as they begin to colour, stir frequently. The colour of the onions gradually turns golden and then more rapidly to brown, so take care to stir constantly at this stage so they do not burn on the base.

2 Fry the onions briskly for a few minutes, stirring regularly, and then reduce the heat and cook gently for 45–60 minutes.

3 When the onions are a rich mahogany brown, add the beef stock and a little seasoning. Simmer, partially covered, for 30 minutes, then taste and adjust the seasoning according to taste.

4 Preheat the grill and toast the French bread. Spoon the soup into four ovenproof serving dishes and place a piece of bread in each. Sprinkle with the cheese and grill for a few minutes until the cheese has melted.

Melon & Parma Ham Salad with Strawberry Salsa

The savoury-sweet salsa complements the melon and ham beautifully.

Serves 4

INGREDIENTS
1 large melon, cantaloupe, galia
   or charentais
175 g/6 oz Parma or Serrano ham,
   thinly sliced

FOR THE SALSA
225 g/8 oz/2 cups strawberries
5 ml/1 tsp caster sugar
30 ml/2 tbsp groundnut or sunflower oil
15 ml/1 tbsp orange juice
2.5 ml/½ tsp finely grated orange rind
2.5 ml/½ tsp finely grated fresh
   root ginger
salt and freshly ground black pepper

1 Halve the melon and take the seeds out with a spoon. Cut the rind away with a paring knife, then slice the melon flesh thickly. Chill until you are ready to serve.

2 To make the salsa, hull the strawberries and cut them into large dice. Place in a small mixing bowl with the sugar and crush lightly to release their juices. Add the oil, orange juice, rind and ginger. Season with salt and a generous twist of black pepper.

3 Arrange the melon on a serving plate, lay the ham over the top and serve with a bowl of the salsa.

Papaya & Avocado Salad

Serves 4

INGREDIENTS

2 ripe avocados, peeled, stoned and cut into
    8 slices lengthways
1 ripe papaya, peeled, seeded and cut into
    16 slices lengthways (seeds reserved)
1 large sweet orange, peeled
    and segmented
475 ml/16 fl oz/2 cups small rocket leaves
1 small red onion, thinly sliced and
    separated into rings

FOR THE DRESSING
50 ml/2 fl oz/¼ cup olive oil
30 ml/2 tbsp lemon or lime juice
salt and freshly ground black pepper

1 To make the dressing, mix all the ingredients together in a bowl. Stir in the reserved papaya seeds.

2 Assemble the salad on four individual serving plates. Alternate slices of avocado and papaya and add the orange sections and a small round of rocket topped with onion rings. Spoon on the dressing and serve.

COOK'S TIP: Avocado slices blacken very quickly, so to enjoy this beautiful salad at its most attractive, prepare it just before you are ready to serve.

Grilled Goat's Cheese Salad

The tangy flavour of goat's cheese contrasts with the mild salad leaves.

Serves 4

INGREDIENTS
4 slices French bread
2 firm round whole goat's cheeses, such as
    Crottin de Chavignol (about 65–115 g/
    2½–4 oz each), cut in half horizontally
extra virgin olive oil, for drizzling
175 g/6 oz/5–6 cups mixed salad leaves,
    including soft and bitter varieties
snipped fresh chives, to garnish

FOR THE VINAIGRETTE DRESSING
1 garlic clove
5 ml/1 tsp Dijon mustard
5 ml/1 tsp white wine vinegar
5 ml/1 tsp dry white wine
45 ml/3 tbsp extra virgin olive oil
salt and freshly ground black pepper

1 Peel and cut the garlic clove in half.
To make the dressing, rub a large salad
bowl with the cut side of the garlic.
Add the remaining ingredients to the
bowl and whisk well to combine.

2 Preheat the grill to hot. Toast the
bread on one side, turn over and place
a piece of cheese, cut side up, on each
slice. Drizzle with oil and grill until
lightly browned.

3 Add the mixed salad leaves to the
salad bowl and toss to coat them
with the dressing. Divide the leaves
among four serving plates, top each
with a goat's cheese croûton and
serve immediately, garnished with
fresh chives.

Smoked Trout Salad

A creamy horseradish dressing unites smoked trout and new potatoes.

Serves 4

INGREDIENTS
675 g/1½ lb new potatoes
4 smoked trout fillets
115 g/4 oz mixed salad leaves
4 slices dark rye bread,
   cut into fingers
4 tomatoes
salt and freshly ground black pepper

FOR THE DRESSING
60 ml/4 tbsp creamed horseradish
60 ml/4 tbsp groundnut oil
15 ml/1 tbsp white wine vinegar
10 ml/2 tsp caraway seeds

1 Bring the potatoes to the boil in a pan of salted water and simmer for 20 minutes, then drain. Remove the skin and any bones from the trout.

2 To make the dressing, place all the ingredients in a screw-top jar and shake vigorously. Season the salad leaves and moisten with the dressing. Distribute among four plates.

3 Flake the trout and halve the potatoes and tomatoes. Scatter, together with the rye fingers, over the salad leaves and toss to mix. Season and serve.

Warm Prawn Salad with Spicy Marinade

The ingredients can be prepared in advance; if you do this, cook the prawns and bacon just before serving, spoon over the salad and serve with hot herb-and-garlic bread.

Serves 8

INGREDIENTS
225 g/8 oz large cooked shelled prawns
225 g/8 oz smoked streaky
   bacon, chopped
mixed salad leaves
30 ml/2 tbsp snipped
   fresh chives

FOR THE LEMON AND CHILLI MARINADE
1 garlic clove, crushed
finely grated rind of 1 lemon
15 ml/1 tbsp lemon juice
60 ml/4 tbsp olive oil
1.5 ml/¼ tsp chilli paste, or a large pinch
   of dried ground chilli
15 ml/1 tbsp light soy sauce
salt and freshly ground
   black pepper

1 To make the marinade, mix the garlic, lemon rind and juice, 45 ml/ 3 tbsp of the oil, the chilli paste or ground chilli, soy sauce and seasoning in a small bowl. Put the prawns in a larger bowl, pour over the marinade and stir to mix well. Cover with clear film and leave to marinate for at least 1 hour.

2 Gently cook the bacon in the remaining oil until crisp. Drain on kitchen paper.

3 Wash and dry the salad leaves and tear into bite-size pieces. Arrange them in individual serving bowls or on plates.

4 Just before serving, put the prawns with their marinade into a large frying pan, bring to the boil, add the bacon and cook for 1 minute. Spoon over the salad and sprinkle with snipped chives. Serve immediately.

Pan-fried Chicken Liver Salad

This Florentine-style salad uses *vin santo*, a sweet dessert wine from Tuscany, but this is not essential – any dessert wine will do, or alternatively a sweet or cream sherry may be used.

Serves 4

INGREDIENTS
75 g/3 oz baby spinach leaves
75 g/3 oz lollo rosso leaves
75 ml/5 tbsp olive oil
15 ml/1 tbsp butter
225 g/8 oz chicken livers, trimmed and
thinly sliced
45ml/3 tbsp *vin santo*
50–75 g/2–3 oz Parmesan cheese,
shaved into curls
salt and freshly ground
black pepper

2 Heat 30 ml/2 tbsp of the oil with the butter in a large, heavy-based frying pan. When foaming, add the chicken livers and toss over a medium to high heat for 5 minutes or until browned on the outside but still pink in the centre. Remove from the heat.

1 Wash and dry the baby spinach leaves and lollo rosso. Tear the leaves into smaller pieces and place in a large bowl. Season with salt and freshly ground black pepper to taste and toss gently to mix.

3 Remove the livers from the pan with a slotted spoon, drain them on kitchen paper, then place on top of the salad leaves.

4 Return the pan to a medium heat, add the remaining oil and the *vin santo* and stir until sizzling.

5 Pour the hot dressing over the salad and toss to coat. Transfer to a serving bowl and sprinkle over the Parmesan. Serve at once.

Smoked Salmon & Lemon Pâté

Making this pâté in individual ramekins wrapped in extra smoked salmon gives an extra-special presentation.

Serves 4

INGREDIENTS
350 g/12 oz thinly sliced
    smoked salmon
150 ml/¼ pint/⅔ cup double cream
finely grated rind and juice of 1 lemon
salt and freshly ground
    black pepper
Melba toast, to serve

2 In a food processor fitted with a metal blade, process the rest of the salmon with the seasoning, double cream and lemon rind and juice.

1 Line four small ramekin dishes with clear film. Line the dishes with 115 g/4 oz of the smoked salmon cut into strips long enough to flop over the edges.

COOK'S TIP: Process the salmon in short bursts until it is just smooth. Don't over-process the pâté or it will thicken too much.

3 Pack the lined ramekins with the smoked salmon pâté and wrap the loose strips of salmon over the top. Cover the pâté and chill for 30 minutes, then turn out of the moulds and serve with Melba toast.

Monkfish Parcels

These unusual little fish dumplings, served with a fresh tomato dressing, make a light-as-air starter.

Serves 4

INGREDIENTS
175 g/6 oz/1½ cups strong plain flour
2 eggs
115 g/4 oz skinless monkfish
    fillet, diced
grated rind of 1 lemon
1 garlic clove, chopped
1 small red chilli, seeded and sliced
45 ml/3 tbsp chopped
    fresh parsley
30 ml/2 tbsp single cream
salt and freshly ground
    black pepper

FOR THE TOMATO OIL
2 tomatoes, peeled, seeded and
    finely diced
45 ml/3 tbsp extra virgin olive oil
30 ml/2 tbsp fresh lemon juice

1 Place the flour, eggs and 2.5 ml/
½ tsp salt in a food processor and pulse until the mixture forms a soft dough. Knead for 2–3 minutes, then wrap it in clear film. Chill the dough for 20 minutes.

2 Place the monkfish, lemon rind, garlic, chilli and parsley in the clean food processor and process until very finely chopped. Add the cream, with plenty of salt and pepper, and process again to form a very thick purée.

3 To make the tomato oil, stir the diced tomato, olive oil and lemon juice together in a bowl. Add salt to taste. Cover and chill.

4 Roll out the dough on a lightly floured surface and cut out 32 rounds, using a 4 cm/1½ in plain cutter. Divide the filling among half the rounds, then cover with the remaining rounds. Pinch the edges tightly to seal, excluding as much air as possible.

5 Bring a large saucepan of water to simmering point and poach the parcels, in batches, for 2–3 minutes or until they rise to the surface. Drain the parcels and serve them hot, drizzled with the tomato oil.

COOK'S TIP: If the dough mixture becomes too sticky to work with, sprinkle a little flour into the food processor bowl and process briefly again.

Thai Fish Cakes

Bursting with the flavours of chillies and lime, these small fish cakes
are a wonderful way to start a meal.

Serves 4

INGREDIENTS
450 g/1 lb white fish fillets, such as
    cod or haddock
3 spring onions, sliced
30 ml/2 tbsp chopped
    fresh coriander
30 ml/2 tbsp Thai red
    curry paste
1 green chilli, seeded and chopped
10 ml/2 tsp grated lime rind
15 ml/1 tbsp lime juice
30 ml/2 tbsp groundnut oil
salt
crisp lettuce leaves, shredded spring onions,
    red chilli slices, coriander sprigs and lime
    wedges, to serve

2 Using lightly floured hands, divide
the mixture into 16 pieces and shape
each one into a small cake about
4 cm/1½ in across. Place the fish cakes
on a plate, cover with clear film and
chill for about 2 hours until firm.

1 Cut the fish into chunks, then place
in a food processor or blender. Add the
spring onions, coriander, red curry
paste, green chilli, lime rind and juice.
Season to taste with salt. Process until
finely minced.

3 Heat a wok over a high heat until
hot. Add the oil and swirl it around.
Fry the fish cakes, a few at a time, for
6–8 minutes, turning them carefully
until evenly browned. Drain each
batch on kitchen paper and keep hot
while cooking the remainder.

4 Serve the fish cakes on a bed of crisp lettuce leaves with shredded spring onions, red chilli slices, coriander sprigs and lime wedges.

COOK'S TIP: If you prefer, the fish cakes can be grilled instead of fried in a wok.

Grilled Mussels with Parsley & Parmesan

This is sure to become one of your all-time favourite starters – as the mussels are grilling, they release an irresistible aroma.

Serves 4

INGREDIENTS
450 g/1 lb fresh mussels
45 ml/3 tbsp water
15 ml/1 tbsp melted butter
15 ml/1 tbsp olive oil
45 ml/3 tbsp grated
   Parmesan cheese
30 ml/2 tbsp chopped
   fresh parsley
2 garlic cloves, finely chopped
2.5 ml/½ tsp coarsely ground
   black pepper

1 Scrub the mussels thoroughly, scraping off any barnacles with a round-bladed knife and pulling out the gritty beards. Sharply tap any open mussels and discard any that fail to close. Place the mussels and water in a large saucepan. Cover and steam for 5 minutes or until the mussels have opened.

2 Drain the mussels, discarding any that remain closed. Snap the top shell off each, leaving the mussel still attached to the bottom shell.

3 Carefully balance the mussels in their shells in a flameproof dish, packing them closely together so that they are supported and stay level.

4 Preheat the grill to high. In a small bowl, mix together the melted butter, olive oil, Parmesan, fresh parsley, garlic and freshly ground black pepper.

5 Using a teaspoon, place a small amount of the cheese mixture on top of each mussel. Grill for 2–3 minutes or until the mussels are sizzling and golden brown.

6 Serve the mussels in their shells, but remember to provide napkins for your guests to wipe their chins!

COOK'S TIP: If you can't get fresh mussels, shelled frozen mussels will work well. Thaw and drain, then place in four individual heatproof dishes. Top with the parsley mixture and grill for the same time. Serve the mussels with teaspoons and offer plenty of bread to mop up the juices.

Tiger Prawn Skewers with Walnut Pesto

An unusual starter, which can be prepared in advance and kept in the fridge until you're ready to cook it.

Serves 4

INGREDIENTS
12–16 large raw unshelled tiger prawns
50 g/2 oz/½ cup walnut pieces
60 ml/4 tbsp chopped fresh flat leaf parsley
60 ml/4 tbsp chopped fresh basil
2 garlic cloves, chopped
45 ml/3 tbsp grated Parmesan cheese
30 ml/2 tbsp extra virgin olive oil
30 ml/2 tbsp walnut oil
salt and freshly ground black pepper

3 Add half the pesto to the prawns in the bowl, toss them well to ensure they are thoroughly combined and then cover the bowl and chill for a minimum of 1 hour; or leave them to marinate overnight.

1 Peel the prawns, removing the head but leaving on the tail section. De-vein and then put the prawns in a large bowl.

2 To make the pesto, place the walnuts, parsley, basil, garlic, Parmesan and oils in a food processor or blender and process until very finely chopped. Season with salt and pepper.

4 Thread the prawns on to skewers, making two insertions through each, as shown. Cook them on a hot barbecue for 3–4 minutes, turning once. Serve the prawns with the remaining walnut pesto.

Oysters Rockefeller

A luxurious starter that proves these shellfish, traditionally enjoyed raw, can be just as delicious when cooked.

Serves 6

INGREDIENTS
450 g/1 lb spinach leaves
40 g/1½ oz/½ cup chopped spring onions
50 g/2 oz/½ cup chopped celery
25 g/1 oz/½ cup chopped fresh parsley
1 garlic clove
2 canned anchovy fillets, drained
50 g/2 oz/4 tbsp butter
25 g/1 oz/½ cup dry breadcrumbs
5 ml/1 tsp Worcestershire sauce
30 ml/2 tbsp anise-flavoured liqueur
 (Pernod or Ricard)
2.5 ml/½ tsp salt
hot pepper sauce
36 unshelled oysters
fine strips of lemon rind, to garnish

2 Put the spinach, spring onions, celery, parsley, garlic and anchovy fillets in a food processor and process until finely chopped.

3 Heat the butter in a frying pan. Add the spinach mixture, breadcrumbs, Worcestershire sauce, liqueur, salt and hot pepper sauce to taste. Cook for 1–2 minutes. Allow to cool, until ready to use.

4 Preheat the oven to 230°C/450°F/ Gas 8. Line a baking sheet with crumpled foil. Open the oysters and remove the top shells. Arrange them, side by side, on the foil (it will keep them upright). Spoon the spinach mixture over the oysters, smoothing the tops with the back of the spoon.

1 Wash the spinach well. Drain and place in a heavy saucepan. Cover and cook over a low heat for a few minutes until just wilted. Remove from the heat. When the spinach is cool enough to handle, squeeze it to remove excess water.

5 Bake the oysters for about 20 minutes until they are piping hot. Serve immediately, garnished with fine strips of lemon rind.

COOK'S TIP: To open an oyster, push the point of an oyster knife about 1 cm/½ in into the "hinge". Push down firmly. The lid of the oyster should pop open.

Assorted Tempura

Tempura is a delicate, delicious dish of savoury fritters in light batter.

Serves 4–6

INGREDIENTS
115 g/4 oz mooli, finely grated (optional)
115 g/4 oz unpeeled sweet potato, sliced and
   soaked in cold water for 5 minutes
75 g/3 oz carrot, cut into matchsticks
4 shiitake mushrooms, stems removed
50 g/2 oz French beans, trimmed
1 red pepper, seeded and sliced into
   2 cm/¾ in thick strips
½ squid body sack, cut into
   3 cm/1¼ in thick strips
8 large tiger prawns, heads removed and
   de-veined, but tails left intact
oil, for deep frying
flour, for coating

FOR THE TEMPURA DIP
200 ml/7 fl oz/scant 1 cup water
45 ml/3 tbsp mirin
10 g/¼ oz bonito flakes
45 ml/3 tbsp soy sauce

FOR THE TEMPURA BATTER
½ egg, beaten
90 ml/6 tbsp iced water
75 g/3 oz/¾ cup plain flour
2.5 ml/½ tsp baking powder
2 ice cubes

1 Bring all the dip ingredients to the boil, then cool and strain. Divide among individual bowls. Place the grated mooli, if using, in a fine sieve and set aside to drain.

2 When all the vegetables and seafood are prepared, make the batter. Put the egg in a bowl and add the iced water, flour and baking powder all at once. Stir only two or three times, leaving some free flour unblended and ignoring any lumps. Add the ice cubes.

3 Heat the oil for deep frying to 185°C/365°F. Dust the tiger prawns lightly with flour and, holding them by the tail, quickly dip them into the batter, then slowly lower them into the hot oil. Fry all the prawns and strips of squid in this way, then drain and reduce the temperature of the oil to 170°C/340°F.

4 Dip the prepared vegetables straight into the batter and cook in the same way as the prawns and squid. Dip the carrots and beans in small bunches. Dip only the undersides of the mushrooms. Drain well.

5 Place the tempura on individual serving plates and serve immediately with the bowls of dip. Don't forget to supply napkins in case your guests choose to eat the tempura with their fingers.

COOK'S TIP: If you find that the batter starts to thin while you are dipping the seafood and vegetables, sprinkle 15 ml/1 tbsp flour over it without mixing it in.

Chicken & Pistachio Pâté

This simplified version of a classic of French charcuterie can be made using a whole boned bird or chicken pieces. It is a versatile dish that can form part of an elegant picnic or a cold buffet.

Serves 10–12

INGREDIENTS
900 g/2 lb boneless chicken meat
1 skinless boneless chicken breast
  (about 175 g/6 oz)
25 g/1 oz/½ cup fresh
  white breadcrumbs
120 ml/4 fl oz/½ cup whipping cream
1 egg white
4 spring onions, finely chopped
1 garlic clove, finely chopped
75 g/3 oz cooked ham, cut into
  1 cm/½ in cubes
50 g/2 oz/½ cup shelled pistachio nuts
45 ml/3 tbsp chopped fresh tarragon
pinch of grated nutmeg
3.5 ml/¾ tsp salt
7.5 ml/1½ tsp freshly ground
  black pepper
green salad, to serve

1 Trim all the fat, tendons and connective tissue from the 900 g/2 lb chicken meat and cut into 5 cm/ 2 in cubes. Put in a food processor fitted with a metal blade and pulse to chop the meat to a smooth purée, in two or three batches (depending on the capacity of your processor).

2 Preheat the oven to 180°C/350°F/ Gas 4. Cut the chicken breast fillet into 1 cm/½ in cubes.

3 In a large mixing bowl, soak the breadcrumbs in the cream. Add the puréed chicken, cubed chicken and all the remaining pâté ingredients. Using a wooden spoon or your fingers, mix until very well combined.

4 Lay out a piece of extra-wide, strong foil about 45 cm/18 in long on a work surface and lightly brush with oil to make a 30 cm/12 in square in the centre. Spoon the mixture on to this to form a log shape about 30 cm/ 12 in long and 9 cm/3½ in thick across the width of the foil. Bring together the long sides of the foil and fold over securely to enclose. Twist the ends of the foil and tie with string.

5 Transfer to a baking dish and bake for 1½ hours. Leave to cool in the dish, then chill. Remove the foil. Serve the pâté sliced with green salad.

Chicken Roulades

These chicken rolls can be served hot with the creamy chive sauce or served cold, cut into slices.

Serves 4

INGREDIENTS
4 skinless boneless chicken thighs
115 g/4 oz chopped frozen spinach
15 g/½ oz/1 tbsp butter
25 g/1 oz/2 tbsp pine nuts
pinch of freshly grated nutmeg
25 g/1 oz/½ cup fresh
    white breadcrumbs
4 rashers rindless streaky bacon
30 ml/2 tbsp olive oil
150 ml/¼ pint/⅔ cup white wine or
    chicken stock
10 ml/2 tsp cornflour
30 ml/2 tbsp single cream
15 ml/1 tbsp chopped fresh chives
salt and freshly ground
    black pepper
salad leaves, to serve

3 Divide the filling among the chicken pieces and roll up neatly. Wrap a rasher of bacon around each piece and secure with string.

4 Heat the oil in a large frying pan and brown the rolls all over. Drain and place in a shallow ovenproof dish.

5 Pour over the wine or stock, cover and bake for 15–20 minutes or until tender. Transfer the chicken roulades to a serving plate and remove the string. Strain the cooking liquid into a clean saucepan.

1 Preheat the oven to 180°C/350°F/ Gas 4. Place the chicken thighs between clear film and flatten with a rolling pin.

2 Put the frozen spinach and butter into a medium saucepan, heat gently until the spinach has defrosted, then increase the heat and cook rapidly, stirring occasionally, until all the moisture has been driven off. Add the pine nuts, grated nutmeg, fresh breadcrumbs, salt and freshly ground black pepper.

6 Mix the cornflour to a smooth paste with a little cold water and add to the cooking juices in the pan, along with the single cream. Bring the mixture to the boil to thicken, stirring all the time to prevent lumps forming. Adjust the seasoning and add the fresh chives. Pour the sauce round the chicken roulades and serve them immediately with salad leaves.

Dolmades

These dainty vine-leaf parcels are very popular in Mediterranean countries. They are traditionally served as part of a Greek *meze*.

Serves 4

INGREDIENTS
8 vine leaves
green and red pepper salad, to serve

FOR THE FILLING
15 ml/1 tbsp olive oil
115 g/4 oz/1 cup minced beef or lamb
30 ml/2 tbsp pine nuts
1 onion, chopped
15 ml/1 tbsp chopped fresh coriander
5 ml/1 tsp ground cumin
15 ml/1 tbsp tomato purée
salt and freshly ground black pepper

FOR THE TOMATO SAUCE
150 ml/¼ pint/⅔ cup passata
150 ml/¼ pint/⅔ cup beef or lamb stock
10 ml/2 tsp caster sugar

2 Stir in the fresh coriander, cumin and tomato purée. Cook for a further 3 minutes and season well.

3 Lay the vine leaves shiny side down on a work surface. Place some of the filling in the centre of each leaf and fold the stalk end over the filling. Roll up the parcel towards the tip of the leaf and place in a lightly greased, flameproof casserole, seam side down. Repeat with the remaining leaves and filling.

1 To make the filling, heat the oil in a pan. Add the minced beef or lamb, pine nuts and onion. Cook for 5 minutes until brown and sealed.

4 To make the sauce, mix together the passata, stock and sugar and pour over the vine leaves. Cover and cook over a moderate heat for 3–4 minutes. Reduce the heat and cook for a further 30 minutes. Serve with green and red pepper salad.

VARIATION: If vine leaves are unavailable, use cabbage leaves briefly dropped in boiling water until wilted.

Carpaccio with Rocket

This is a fine Italian dish of raw beef marinated in lemon juice and olive oil. It is traditionally served with flakes of fresh Parmesan cheese. Use very fresh meat of the best quality.

Serves 4

INGREDIENTS
1 garlic clove
1½ lemons
50 ml/2 fl oz/¼ cup extra virgin
    olive oil
2 bunches rocket
4 very thin slices beef
115 g/4 oz Parmesan cheese
salt and freshly ground
    black pepper

1 Cut the garlic clove in half and rub the cut side all over the inside of a small bowl. Squeeze the lemons into the bowl. Whisk in the olive oil and season to taste. Allow to stand for at least 15 minutes before using.

2 Carefully wash the rocket. Tear off and discard any thick stalks. Spin or pat dry with kitchen paper.

3 Arrange the rocket in an attractive circular pattern around the edge of a large serving platter. Alternatively, divide the rocket among four individual serving plates and arrange the same way.

4 Place the sliced beef in the centre of the rocket leaves on the platter or plates and pour on the prepared dressing, spreading it evenly over the slices of meat. Shave the Parmesan cheese thinly and arrange the shavings on top of the meat slices, again forming a circular pattern. Serve the carpaccio at once.

COOK'S TIP: Since this recipe contains uncooked meat it is advisable to buy organically reared meat from a specialist butcher. Ask the butcher to slice it freshly to your requirements, to ensure that you obtain wafer-thin slices.

Beef & Cheese Tartlets

These delicious individual tartlets are seasoned with thyme and leeks and topped with a tangy cheese sauce to excite the palate.

Serves 4

INGREDIENTS
225 g/8 oz shortcrust pastry
fresh parsley and tomato slices, to garnish
salad, to serve

FOR THE FILLING
7.5 ml/1½ tsp oil
115 g/4 oz/1 cup minced beef
7.5 ml/1½ tsp chopped fresh thyme
1 small leek, sliced
salt and freshly ground black pepper

FOR THE CHEESE SAUCE
15 g/½ oz/1 tbsp butter
15 g/½ oz/1 tbsp plain flour
120 ml/4 fl oz/½ cup milk
25 g/1 oz/¼ cup grated mature
    Cheddar cheese
2.5 ml/½ tsp mustard

1 Preheat the oven to 190°C/375°F/ Gas 5. Roll out the pastry and use to line four 7.5 cm/3 in tartlet tins. Bake blind for 15 minutes.

2 To make the filling, heat the oil in a large pan and fry the minced beef, thyme and leek for 10 minutes. Season to taste and drain, if necessary.

3 To make the cheese sauce, melt the butter in a pan. Add the flour and cook for 1 minute. Stir in the milk and cheese. Bring to the boil, stirring. Add the mustard and seasoning.

4 Spoon the mince mixture into the base of the cases, top with cheese sauce and cook for 10–15 minutes in the oven. Garnish with parsley and tomato slices and serve with salad.

Stuffed Peppers

Stuffed peppers make a tasty and attractive starter. Orange peppers may be used as well to make the colour combination even more dramatic.

Serves 6

INGREDIENTS

6 mixed peppers (red, yellow and green)
30 ml/2 tbsp olive oil
1 large onion, finely chopped
3–4 spring onions, finely chopped
250 g/9 oz minced lamb
2 garlic cloves, crushed (optional)
50 g/2 oz/¼ cup yellow split peas
75 g/3 oz/½ cup cooked rice
30 ml/2 tbsp finely chopped
   fresh parsley
30 ml/2 tbsp finely chopped fresh mint
30 ml/2 tbsp finely snipped fresh chives
5 ml/1 tsp ground cinnamon
juice of 2 lemons
30 ml/2 tbsp tomato purée (optional)
400 g/14 oz can chopped tomatoes
knob of butter
salt and freshly ground black pepper
yogurt and pitta bread or naan, to serve

1 Cut off the pepper tops and set aside. Remove the seeds and cores and trim the bases so they stand upright. Cook in boiling salted water for 5 minutes, then drain, rinse under cold water and set aside.

2 Heat the oil in a large pan and fry the onion and spring onions for about 4–5 minutes until golden brown. Add the meat and fry until well browned. Stir in the garlic if using.

3 Place the split peas in a small pan with enough water to cover, bring to the boil and simmer gently for 12–15 minutes until soft. Drain.

4 Stir the split peas, cooked rice, parsley, mint, chives, cinnamon, half the lemon juice and the tomato purée, if using, into the meat. Season. Spoon the mixture into the peppers and top with the reserved lids.

5 Pour the chopped tomatoes into a pan in which the peppers will fit quite snugly, and add the remaining lemon juice and butter. Arrange the peppers in the pan with the stems upwards. Bring to the boil, cover tightly and cook over a low heat for 40–45 minutes until tender.

6 Serve the peppers with the tomato sauce, accompanied by yogurt and warm pitta bread or naan.

Stuffed Artichokes

The amount of stuffing needed for this dish depends on the size of the artichokes – if they are small, you could serve one per person. If you can find them, the purple-tinged artichokes have the finest flavour.

Serves 4

INGREDIENTS
2 globe artichokes, prepared
lemon juice

FOR THE STUFFING
25 g/1 oz/2 tbsp butter
2–3 small leeks, sliced
2-3 bacon rashers, chopped (optional)
75 g/3 oz Mozzarella cheese, cut into
    small cubes
25–40 g/1–1½ oz/½–¾ cup fresh brown
    or white breadcrumbs
5 ml/1 tsp chopped
    fresh basil
salt and freshly ground
    black pepper
fresh basil leaves,
    to garnish

1 Place the artichokes in a large saucepan of salted water. Bring the water to the boil, cover and cook the artichokes for 35–40 minutes or until a lower leaf comes away easily when gently pulled.

VARIATION: For a vegetarian version of this dish simply omit the bacon and increase the amount of Mozzarella cheese and leeks.

2 To make the stuffing, melt the butter in a saucepan and gently fry the leeks for 4 minutes. Add the bacon and fry until golden brown. Remove the pan from the heat and stir in the Mozzarella cubes, breadcrumbs, basil and seasoning to taste.

3 Drain the artichokes upside down and cool. Cut them in half from top to bottom. Remove the inner leaves, discard the choke and sprinkle the inside and base liberally with lemon juice to avoid discoloration.

4 Preheat the grill to moderately hot. Spoon a little stuffing into each artichoke half and place in a single layer in an ovenproof dish. Grill for 5–6 minutes until the stuffing is golden. Serve garnished with basil leaves.

Asparagus with Orange Sauce

White asparagus is considered a delicacy by many although it doesn't have the intense flavour of the green variety. White spears and large green ones are best peeled, starting from just below the tip.

Serves 6

INGREDIENTS
175 g/6 oz/¾ cup unsalted
   butter, diced
3 egg yolks
15 ml/1 tbsp cold water
15 ml/1 tbsp lemon juice
grated rind and juice of
   1 unwaxed orange
30–36 thick green or white asparagus
   spears, trimmed to the same length
salt and cayenne pepper
a few shreds of orange rind,
   to garnish

2 In a heatproof bowl set over a pan of barely simmering water, whisk together the egg yolks, water, lemon juice, 15 ml/1 tbsp of the orange juice and salt until the mixture starts to thicken and the whisk begins to leave tracks on the base of the pan. Remove from the heat.

1 Melt the diced, unsalted butter in a small saucepan set over a low heat. Stir constantly and do not allow to boil. With a spoon, skim off any foam that forms on the top, and set the melted butter aside until you are ready to add it to the sauce.

3 Whisk in the melted butter, drop by drop, until the sauce thickens further, then pour it in more quickly, leaving behind the milky solids. Whisk in the orange rind and 30–60 ml/ 2–4 tbsp of the juice. Season with salt and cayenne pepper and keep warm, stirring occasionally.

4 Fill a deep frying pan with 5 cm/ 2 in water and bring to the boil over a medium-high heat. Add the asparagus and return to the boil. Simmer for 4–7 minutes until just tender.

5 Carefully transfer the cooked asparagus spears to a large colander to drain, then lay them on a clean dish towel and pat dry.

6 Arrange the asparagus spears on a large serving platter or on six individual plates and spoon over a little of the orange sauce. Scatter the orange rind over the sauce and serve at once.

COOK'S TIP: This sauce is a type of hollandaise and needs gentle treatment. If the egg yolk mixture thickens too quickly, remove from the heat and plunge the base of the pan into cold water to prevent curdling. The sauce should keep over hot water for 1 hour, but don't let it get too hot.

Aubergine & Tahini Dip

This popular Middle-eastern dish is said to have been invented by the ladies of a sultan's harem – to win his favour.

Serves 4–6

INGREDIENTS
3 aubergines
2 garlic cloves, crushed
60 ml/4 tbsp tahini
juice of 2 lemons
15 ml/1 tbsp paprika, plus extra to garnish
salt and freshly ground
    black pepper
chopped fresh parsley, olive oil and a few
    olives, to garnish
crudités or pitta bread, to serve

1 Preheat the oven to 190°C/375°F/ Gas 5. Slit the skins of the aubergines, place on a large baking sheet and bake for 30–40 minutes until the skins begin to split.

2 When the aubergines are cool enough to handle, place them on a chopping board. Carefully peel away and discard the skins.

3 Place the aubergine flesh in a food processor or blender. Add the garlic, tahini, lemon juice, paprika and salt and pepper. Blend to a smooth paste, adding about 15–30 ml/1–2 tbsp water if it is too thick.

4 Spoon into a serving dish and make a hollow in the centre. Garnish with paprika, chopped parsley, a drizzle of olive oil and olives. Serve with a selection of crudités or hot pitta bread.

Stuffed Mushrooms

This is a classic mushroom dish, strongly flavoured with garlic. Use flat mushrooms or, if you are lucky enough to get them, field mushrooms.

Serves 4

INGREDIENTS
450 g/1 lb large, flat mushrooms
butter, for greasing
about 75 ml/5 tbsp olive oil
2 garlic cloves, very
    finely chopped
45 ml/3 tbsp finely chopped
    fresh parsley
40–50 g/1½–2 oz/¾–1 cup fresh
    white breadcrumbs
salt and freshly ground
    black pepper
flat leaf parsley sprig,
    to garnish

1 Preheat the oven to 180°C/350°F/
Gas 4. Cut off the mushroom
stalks and reserve for the stuffing.

COOK'S TIP: The cooking time
for the mushrooms depends on their
size and thickness. If they are fairly
thin, cook for slightly less time.
They should be tender but not too
soft when cooked. If a stronger
garlic flavour is preferred, do not
cook the garlic before adding it to
the breadcrumb mixture.

2 Arrange the mushroom caps, gill
side upwards, in a buttered, shallow
ovenproof dish. Heat 15 ml/1 tbsp of
the olive oil in a frying pan and fry
the garlic briefly.

3 Finely chop the reserved
mushroom stalks and mix with the
parsley and breadcrumbs. Add the
garlic, seasoning and a further 15 ml/
1 tbsp of the oil. Pile a little of the
mixture on each mushroom cap.

4 Add the remaining oil to the dish and cover the mushrooms with buttered greaseproof paper. Bake for about 15–20 minutes, removing the paper for the last 5 minutes. Garnish with flat leaf parsley and serve.

Twice-baked Goat's Cheese Soufflés

A good chef's trick is to reheat small baked soufflés out of their ramekins. They puff up again and the outsides become crispy.

Serves 6

INGREDIENTS
25 g/1 oz/2 tbsp butter
25 g/1 oz/¼ cup plain flour
300 ml/½ pint/1¼ cups hot milk
pinch of cayenne pepper
squeeze of lemon juice
115 g/4 oz semi-hard goat's
    cheese, crumbled
2 eggs, separated
melted butter, for brushing
25 g/1 oz/½ cup dried breadcrumbs
25 g/1 oz/¼ cup ground hazelnuts
    or walnuts
2 egg whites
salt and freshly ground
    black pepper
salad, to serve

1 Melt the butter in a small saucepan and stir in the flour. Cook for 1 minute, stirring, then gradually whisk in the hot milk to make a thick white sauce.

2 Simmer the sauce for 1 minute then season with cayenne pepper, lemon juice, salt and freshly ground black pepper. Remove the pan from the heat and stir in the goat's cheese until it melts. Allow to cool slightly, then beat in the egg yolks.

3 Brush the insides of six ramekins with the butter and coat with the breadcrumbs and nuts mixed together. Shake out any excess. Preheat the oven to 190°C/375°F/Gas 5.

4 Whisk the four egg whites to the soft peak stage and carefully fold them into the main mixture, using a figure-of-eight motion. Spoon the mixture into the ramekins.

5 Place the soufflés in a roasting tin half-filled with boiling water and bake for about 12–15 minutes until risen and golden brown. You can, of course, serve them at this stage; otherwise, allow to cool, then chill.

6 To serve twice-baked, reheat the oven to the same temperature. Run a knife round the inside of each ramekin and turn out each soufflé on to a baking sheet. Bake for about 12 minutes. Serve hot with salad.

Sweetcorn Blinis with Dill Cream

A mouthwatering and unusual starter, these blinis are ideally made an hour or two before you serve them, although the batter will stand for longer than that if required.

Serves 6–8

INGREDIENTS
75 g/3 oz/⅔ cup plain flour
75 g/3 oz/⅔ cup wholemeal flour
250 ml/8 fl oz/1 cup buttermilk
4 small eggs, beaten
2.5 ml/½ tsp salt
2.5 ml/½ tsp baking powder
25 g/1 oz/2 tbsp butter, melted
good pinch of bicarbonate of soda
15 ml/1 tbsp hot water
200 g/7 oz can sweetcorn kernels, drained
oil, for brushing

FOR THE DILL CREAM
200 g/7 oz crème fraîche
30 ml/2 tbsp chopped fresh dill
30 ml/2 tbsp snipped fresh chives
salt and freshly ground black pepper
sliced radishes and fresh dill sprigs,
    to garnish

1 Mix the two flours and buttermilk together until completely smooth. Cover and chill for about 8 hours.

2 Beat in the eggs, salt, baking powder and butter. Mix the bicarbonate of soda with the hot water and add this, too, along with the drained sweetcorn kernels.

3 Heat a griddle or heavy-based frying pan until quite hot. Brush with a little oil and drop spoonfuls of the blini mixture on to it. The mixture should start to sizzle immediately.

4 Cook until holes appear on the top and the mixture looks almost set. Using a palette knife, flip the blinis over and cook briefly on the other side. Stack the cooked blinis under a clean dish towel while you use the remaining mixture to make the rest.

5 To make the dill cream, simply blend the crème fraîche with the fresh dill and chives, and the salt and freshly ground black pepper. Serve the blinis with a few spoonfuls of dill cream, garnished with sliced radishes and fresh dill sprigs.

Roast Pepper Terrine

This terrine is perfect for a dinner party because it tastes better if made in advance. The salsa, however, should be prepared on the day of serving. Serve with hot Italian bread: ciabatta is ideal.

Serves 8

INGREDIENTS

8 peppers (red, yellow and orange), roasted under the grill, peeled and seeded
675 g/1½ lb/3 cups Mascarpone cheese
3 eggs, separated
30 ml/2 tbsp each roughly chopped flat leaf parsley and shredded basil
2 large garlic cloves, roughly chopped
2 red, yellow or orange peppers, seeded and roughly chopped
pinch of sugar
30 ml/2 tbsp extra virgin olive oil
10 ml/2 tsp balsamic vinegar
salt and freshly ground black pepper
a few fresh basil sprigs, to garnish

1 Cut seven of the roasted, peeled and seeded peppers lengthways into thin, even-size strips. Leave the remaining roasted pepper whole and reserve for the salsa.

2 Beat the Mascarpone cheese with the egg yolks, parsley, basil, half the garlic and seasoning. In a separate bowl, whisk the egg whites to the soft peak stage, then fold into the cheese and herb mixture.

3 Preheat the oven to 180°C/350°F/ Gas 4. Line the base of a lightly oiled 900 g/2 lb loaf tin. Put one-third of the cheese mixture in the tin and spread the surface level. Arrange half the prepared roasted pepper strips on top of the cheese mixture in an even layer. Repeat the layers until all the cheese mixture and roasted peppers are used.

4 Cover the tin with foil and place in a roasting tin. Pour in enough boiling water to come halfway up the sides of the tin. Bake for 1 hour. Leave the loaf tin to cool in the water bath, then lift it out and chill overnight.

5 A few hours before serving, make the salsa. Place the remaining roasted pepper and fresh peppers in a food processor. Add the remaining garlic and the sugar, oil and vinegar. Set aside a few basil leaves for garnishing and add the rest to the processor. Process until finely chopped. Tip the mixture into a bowl and season. Chill until ready to serve.

6 Turn out the terrine, peel off the paper and slice thickly. Garnish with basil and serve with the salsa.

COOK'S TIP: The roasted peppers will be easier to peel if placed in sealed plastic bags and left until cool enough to handle.

Brandied Roquefort Tarts

Light puff pastry rounds topped with the irresistible combination of brandy and Roquefort cheese.

Serves 6

INGREDIENTS
150 g/5 oz Roquefort cheese
30 ml/2 tbsp brandy
30 ml/2 tbsp olive oil
2 red onions (about 225 g/8 oz total weight),
    thinly sliced
225 g/8 oz puff pastry, thawed,
    if frozen
beaten egg or milk, to glaze
6 walnut halves, chopped
30 ml/2 tbsp snipped fresh chives
salt and freshly ground black pepper
chive knots, to garnish
salad leaves, diced cucumber and thin
    tomato wedges, to serve

1 Crumble the Roquefort into a small bowl, pour the brandy over and leave to marinate for 1 hour. Meanwhile, heat the olive oil in a frying pan and gently fry the sliced onions for 20 minutes, stirring occasionally. Set the pan aside.

2 Preheat the oven to 220°C/425°F/Gas 7. Grease a baking sheet. Roll out the pastry on a floured surface and stamp out six rounds with a 10 cm/4 in fluted cutter. Put the rounds on the baking sheet and prick with a fork.

3 Brush the edges of the pastry with a little beaten egg or milk. Add the walnuts and chives to the onions and season. Divide among the pastry shapes, leaving the edges clear.

4 Spoon the brandied cheese on top and bake for 12–15 minutes until golden. Serve warm, garnished with chive knots, on salad leaves, diced cucumber and thin tomato wedges.

COOK'S TIP: To make the chive knots, tie chives together in threes, with a central knot. Blanch the chives briefly if not very pliable.

Index

First published in 1999 by Lorenz Books © Anness Publishing Limited 1999

Lorenz Books is an imprint of Anness Publishing Limited, Hermes House, 88–89 Blackfriars Road, London SE1 8HA

This edition distributed in Canada by Raincoast Books, 8680 Cambie Street, Vancouver, British Columbia, V6P 6M9

ISBN 0 7548 0273 6

A CIP catalogue record for this book is available from the British Library.

Publisher: Joanna Lorenz
Editor: Valerie Ferguson
Series Designer: Bobbie Colgate Stone
Designer: Andrew Heath
Production Controller: Joanna King

Recipes contributed by: Angela Boggiano, Carla Capalbo, Carole Clements, Roz Denny, Christine France, Silvano Franco, Shirley Gill, Christine Ingram, Soheila Kimberley, Masaki Ko, Sue Maggs, Norma Miller, Jenny Stacey, Liz Trigg, Laura Washburn, Steven Wheeler, Elizabeth Wolf-Cohen, Jeni Wright.

Photography: William Adams-Lingwood, Karl Adamson, Edward Allwright, James Duncan, Michelle Garrett, Amanda Heywood, Janine Hosegood, David Jordan, Don Last, Patrick McLeavey, Michael Michaels, Juliet Piddington.

1 3 5 7 9 10 8 6 4 2

Notes:
For all recipes, quantities are given in both metric and imperial measures and, where appropriate, measures are also given in standard cups and spoons.
Follow one set, but not a mixture, because they are not interchangeable.

Standard spoon and cup measures are level.

1 tsp = 5 ml   1 tbsp =15 ml

1 cup = 250 ml/8 fl oz

Australian standard tablespoons are 20 ml.
Australian readers should use 3 tsp in place of 1 tbsp for measuring small quantities of gelatine, cornflour, salt, etc.

Medium eggs are used unless otherwise stated.

Printed and bound in Singapore